Lara Ladybug

Written by Christine Florie
Illustrated by Danny Brooks Dalby

Children's Press®
A Division of Scholastic Inc.
New York • Toronto • London • Auckland • Sydney
Mexico City • New Delhi • Hong Kong
Danbury, Connecticut

To my family, for their love and support,
and E.R., who made a dream come true
—C.F.

Reading Consultant

Eileen Robinson
Reading Specialist

Library of Congress Cataloging-in-Publication Data
Florie, Christine, 1964-
  Lara Ladybug / written by Christine Florie; illustrated by Danny Brooks Dalby.
    p. cm. – (A Rookie reader)
Summary: A ladybug searches all over for her lost spots.
  ISBN 0-516-25137-6 (lib. bdg.) 0-516-25281-X (pbk.)
  [1. Lost and found possessions—Fiction. 2. Ladybugs–Fiction.] Dalby, Danny Brooks,
ill. II. Title. III. Series.
PZ7.F6646Lar 2004
[E]—dc22

                              2004009323

CHILDREN'S PRESS, and A ROOKIE READER®, and associated logos are trademarks and or
registered trademarks of Scholastic Library Publishing. SCHOLASTIC and associated logos are
trademarks and or registered trademarks of Scholastic Inc.
1 2 3 4 5 6 7 8 9 10 R 14 13 12 11 10 09 08 07 06 05

Lara Ladybug lost her spots.
Where can they be?

Did she leave them in her garden?
Let's see.

Lara Ladybug lost her spots.
Where can they be?

Did she leave them by the lake?
Let's see.

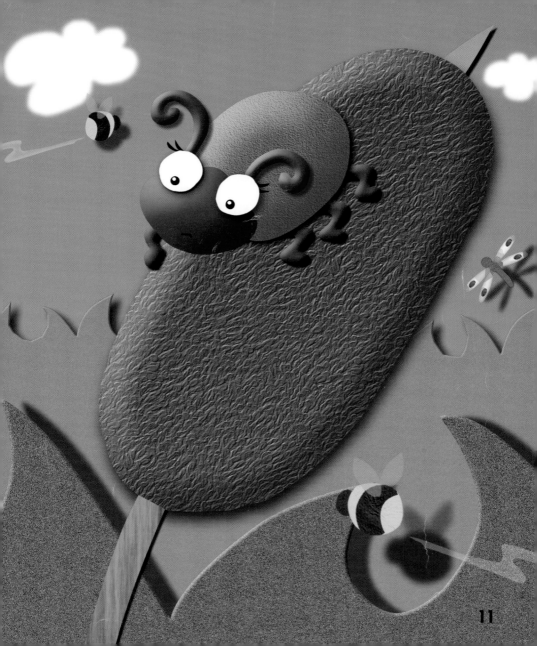

11

Lara Ladybug lost her spots.
Where can they be?

Did she leave them under the tree?
Let's see.

Lara stopped to rest.
What did she see?

Her spots!

One

Two

Three

Word List (29 words)

be	leave	them
by	let's	they
can	lost	three
did	one	to
garden	rest	tree
her	see	two
in	she	under
ladybug	spots	what
lake	stopped	where
Lara	the	

About the Author

Christine Florie is a children's book editor and writer. She lives in Mahopac, New York, with her husband, two daughters, and a black Labrador retriever. When not editing and writing, she enjoys cooking for her family, reading, and spending time with friends. She has also written *Braces for Cori* in the *A Rookie Reader* ® series.

About the Illustrator

Danny Brooks Dalby has been drawing his entire life. His motto is "Read all of your books, eat all of your vegetables, and love your mother."